DATE DUE	

ARTHRITIS

MADELYN KLEIN ANDERSON

ARTHRITIS

93 04046
Franklin Watts
New York / London / Toronto / Sydney / 1989
A Venture Book

Drawings by Janet D'Amato

Photographs courtesy of: Arthritis Foundation:
pp. 26–64; J.A. Preston Corporation: pp. 70–72;
American Occupational Therapy Association: pp. 74–78.

Library of Congress Cataloging-in-Publication Data

Anderson, Madelyn Klein.
Arthritis / by Madelyn Klein Anderson.
p.   cm. — (A Venture book)
Includes index.
Summary: Discusses the many different types of arthritis,
what causes them, how they are treated, and how people
learn to cope with them.
ISBN 0-531-10801-5
1. Arthritis—Juvenile literature.   [1. Arthritis.]   I. Title.
RC933.A495   1989
616.7'22—dc20   89-5745   CIP   AC

*Special thanks to Helene Flapan,
President of the Scleroderma Foundation,
and Dorothy Goldstein,
Medical Director of the New York Chapter
of the Arthritis Foundation.*

CONTENTS

ARTHRITIS

INTRODUCTION

I never indulge in poetics
Unless I am down with rheumatics.

This rueful rhyme was written over twenty-two hundred years ago by a Greek philosopher with a sense of humor and a way with words. In fact, it was the ancient Greeks who coined the word: "rheumaticos."

Rheumatics—rheumatism—plagued the ancient Greeks, plagued the Neanderthal cave dwellers, and plagues us all. Everyone knows at least one of its many forms somewhere in the course of a lifetime, mostly as arthritis.

Rheumatism is an umbrella term, covering all conditions involving inflammation of bone and its surrounding tissues: muscle, tendons, ligaments, cartilage, and fibrous connective tissue. The largest group of rheumatic conditions occurs in and around a *joint,* the place where two bones meet or "articulate." So modern-day scientists took the Greek "arthron," meaning joint, and "itis," meaning inflammation, and combined them into "arthritis."

Arthritis (pl. *arthritides*) is the inflammation of a joint and of the tissues surrounding the joint. The arthritis family is so large, and other conditions under the rheumatism umbrella are so few, that many medical sources have discarded the use of the rheumatism umbrella altogether. Arthritis is now an umbrella term itself, covering over a hundred arthritides.

There aren't any witty Greek rhymes about arthritis. But there's a great American gospel song about joints: "Your head bone's connected to your neck bone, your neck bone's connected to your shoulder bone, your shoulder bone's connected to your elbow bone . . . ." It goes on and on, descending musical phrases taking you right down to the toes and ascending ones taking you all the way up again. Those "connections" are most of your joints.

You have a lot of joints, and that's good—you need them to move. You walk the way you do because your legs are jointed at hip, knee, ankle, and toes. Your jawbones are jointed and so you can open and close them to eat. Your arms and hands bring food to your mouth because they are jointed. Your spine is jointed so that you have flexibility and mobility. Your fingers are jointed and so you can turn the pages of this book. You can do hundreds of complex motions because you have highly functional joints.

We have joints that glide and joints that go up and down and still others that go back and forth or around. Some are freely movable, like the shoulder that can go back and forth *and* around. Look at some of your movements when you are throwing a ball: your wrist bends, your fingers bend and spread to hold the ball, your elbow brings the ball up, your shoulder moves your arm out and around and into the toss, then your elbow straightens, your wrist and fingers open. . . . A lot of joints are doing their thing.

Your joints don't move themselves, however. Muscles move them. *Muscles* are a special kind of tissue made of cells or fibers that can contract—tighten—and relax—return to their original state. There are three categories of muscle in our bodies: cardiac muscle that forms the heart, smooth muscle that works our internal organs (usually without our conscious knowledge), and skeletal muscle that we move consciously.

It is skeletal muscle that works on our joints (and also in the tongue, pharynx, and the top of the esophagus to move food into our stomachs). Skeletal muscles attach to joints by means of a fibrous connective tissue called a *tendon.*

Bands or sheets of fibrous connective tissue called *ligaments* bind the ends of the bones in the joint and thicken into a capsule that surrounds the joint to protect it. Ligaments help motion, but they also limit the action of the joint so that it doesn't go all over the place and you go out of control.

So now you have two bones meeting, bound and protected by ligaments, and moved by the muscles

The Joints

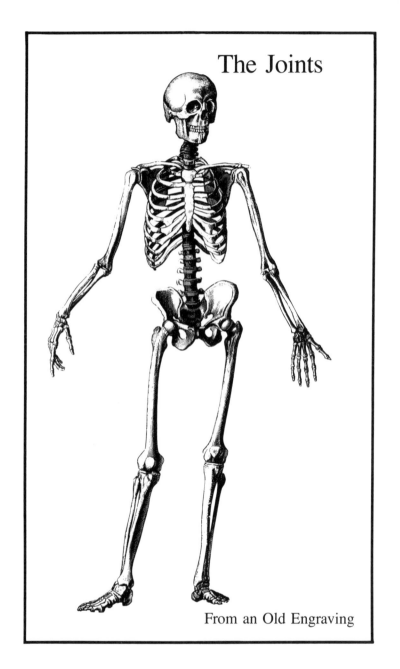

From an Old Engraving

*Bones connect at joints to give our bodies
mobility as well as shape and support.*

of the Human Body

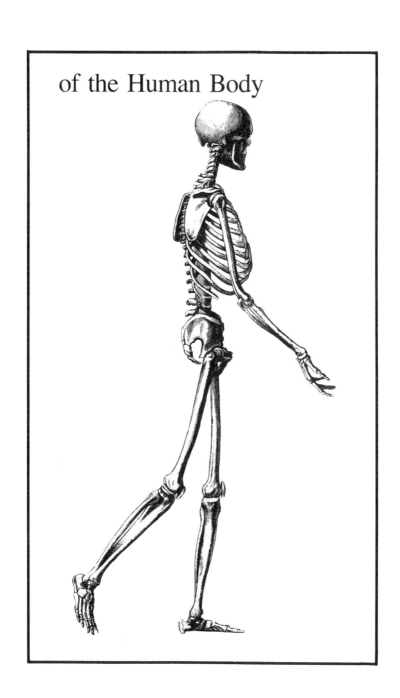

A lot of joints at work

that attach to the bones by tendons. The thought of those two bones grating on one another as they move can send chills through you—and it does in some forms of arthritis. But, fortunately, most joints and tendon insertions into the joint are lined with *synovial membrane,* a thin tissue producing *synovium,* a clear, thick, sticky fluid that smoothes movement of joints much as grease reduces friction between two moving parts of a bicycle or other machine. Many joints also have a kind of cushion between the bones of *articular cartilage,* a firm, jellylike substance to ease friction and also to absorb shock—such as the weight of the body as it changes position.

The knee is a joint with a cartilage cushion. Many football players find themselves sidelined after an awkward fall because the knee joint closed incorrectly and tore a piece of cartilage. The spine is another area where cartilage seems to come in for its share of problems. The spinal column consists of many bones called *vertebrae* (sing. *vertebra*). Most of the vertebrae are joined—that's why you can bend and twist—and like other joints are subject to arthritis. But the cartilage cushions between the vertebrae, called *intervertebral disks,* can sometimes be a special problem. Many people suffer from painful back conditions blamed on a "ruptured disk" or "slipped disk" pinching on a nerve. This is not usually considered arthritis, however, until the now-unprotected vertebrae are affected. But disks don't rupture or slip so easily, and increasing numbers of medical scientists believe these common back problems are really caused by muscle inflammation and nerve spasm. By definition, this would then be considered a rheumatism. You can see how medical discoveries and changing theories can widen or close down umbrella terms like rheumatism and arthritis.

Even the broad classification of arthritis as an immune-system disease is changing in the face of new research evidence. The *immune system* of our bodies is how we respond to internal attack. Inflammation is one of the battle signs, and the continuing inflammation of arthritis is the result of the immune system losing the fight. Now some scientists are reporting a

Type of Joints Classified by Movement They Allow

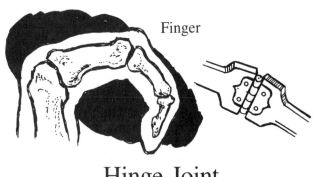

Finger

Hinge Joint

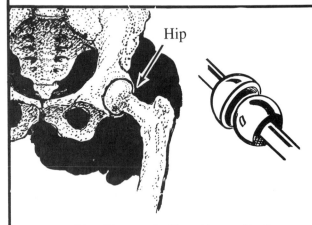

Hip

Ball and Socket Joint

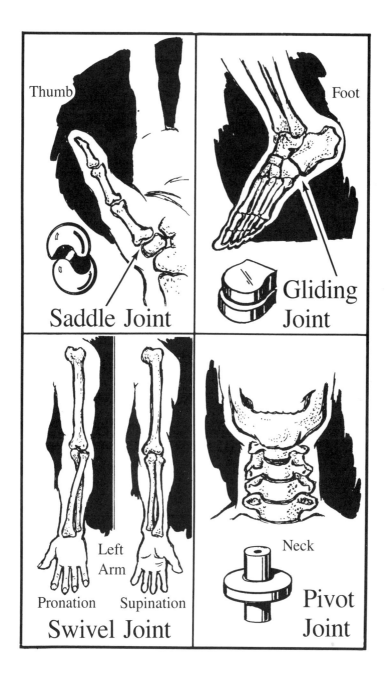

Thumb

Saddle Joint

Foot

Gliding
Joint

Left
Arm

Pronation   Supination

Swivel Joint

Neck

Pivot
Joint

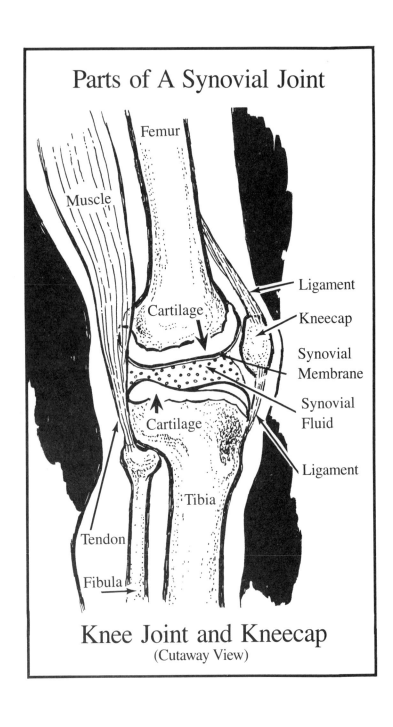

Parts of A Synovial Joint

Femur

Muscle

Ligament

Cartilage

Kneecap

Synovial Membrane

Synovial Fluid

Cartilage

Ligament

Tibia

Tendon

Fibula

Knee Joint and Kneecap
(Cutaway View)

connection between arthritis and the *nervous system* of the body, the brain and spinal cord with its nerves and connections that receive messages and transmit them into action. Their findings are based on research with patients who are *hemiplegic,* paralysed on one side of the body because of interference in the brain with the nerves that supply that side. Arthritis in hemiplegics seems to occur only, or most severely, on the unaffected side of the body rather than both sides. In other words, where nerves do not function, arthritis does not set in, or is far less severe.

Since arthritis has been around for such a very long time, it would seem that we should be certain about its basis. But arthritis research does not go on with the magnitude, intensity, and speed devoted to AIDS, for example. Arthritis is not a killer, except in rare instances, and there's no sense of tremendous urgency about eliminating it. It may not even be possible. Instead, research is aimed at treatment of the

The kneecap is not part of the joint but is shown here because it is an important part of the knee. The knee also has more layers of muscle and more tendons and ligaments, but this cutaway view makes it easier to see its structure and the typical elements of a synovial joint.

The Spinal Column

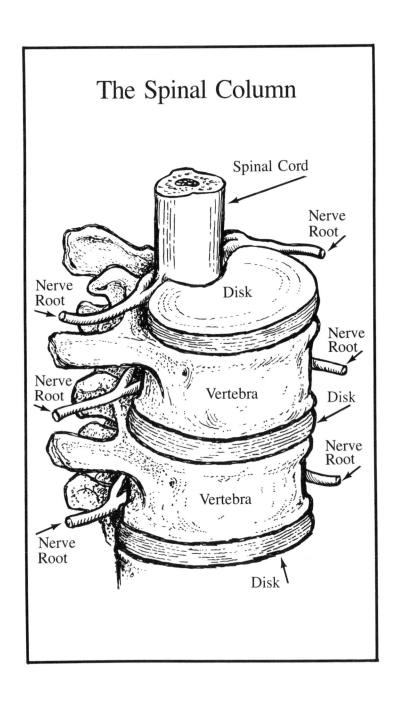

Spinal Cord

Nerve Root

Nerve Root

Disk

Nerve Root

Nerve Root

Vertebra

Disk

Nerve Root

Vertebra

Nerve Root

Disk

symptoms arthritis presents. Arthritis is painful. Some arthritides can be deforming, can seriously undermine function, can cripple.

To better understand the various symptoms, causes, and effects of arthritis, we'll remove the jumbo umbrellas of rheumatism and arthritis and open up a few smaller ones over the different types of arthritis: degenerative, inflammatory, infective, metabolic, and our old friend and catch-all, miscellaneous. Like all umbrellas, they tend to bump one another a bit, especially the "in group"—infective and inflammatory. And different umbrellas are used by different sources, because everybody seems to have their own favorite system for classifying the arthritides. Whatever their umbrellas, underneath the arthritides remain the same.

CHAPTER

1

DEGENERATIVE
ARTHRITIS

When people talk about arthritis or rheumatism, they mostly mean osteoarthritis. That is understandable since osteoarthritis is the most prevalent of the arthritides.

Osteoarthritis is degenerative arthritis, a condition in which joint cartilage degenerates or breaks down. New tissue, which grows at the ends of bones, now has no cartilage cap to control it, to keep it shapely and in place. Instead, this new bone forms—or deforms—into strange lips and spurs that grind and grate and get in the way of movement of the joint.

Osteoarthritis is common in older people after years of wear-and-tear that thin the cartilage and the bones. And osteoarthritis can also result from diseases in which there is softening of bone, like Paget's dis-

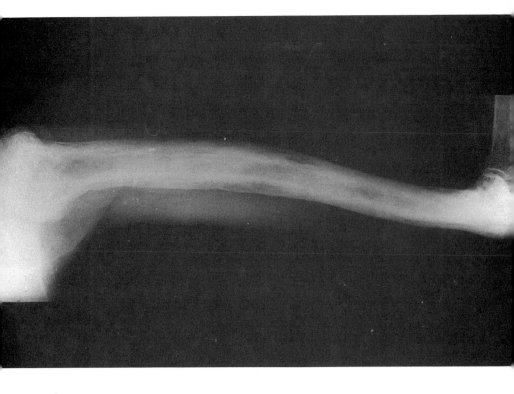

*Bowing of the upper arm,
the humerus, in Paget's disease*

ease, in which the long bones of the body curve like
a bow, or osteoporosis with its bowing of the shoulders called "dowager's hump," or other bone degeneration. Other forms of arthritis can also cause a
secondary osteoarthritis.

Osteoarthritis is not an inevitable problem of ag-
ing. Those who don't suffer from it may have their
heredity and possibly the strength of their immune

systems to thank. Medical science is not quite sure of all the factors that come into play in deciding who gets osteoarthritis and who doesn't. (That's true for most other conditions as well.)

And contrary to what most people think, osteoarthritis does not affect only the older person. Birth defects such as congenital dislocation of the hip can cause osteoarthritis by the time the child reaches the teen years. Perthes' disease, the disintegration of the head of the *femur*—thighbone—in children from 3 to 15, can bring on early osteoarthritis. Children may get osteoarthritis in legbones that do not grow properly. Teenage boys sometimes suffer from a slipping downward of the section where early growth of the femur takes place, causing a painful hip and often a secondary osteoarthritis. *Trauma*—injury—is a major cause of osteoarthritis in the young (and sometimes in the not-so-young). Falls or excessive repetitive motion in some sports can injure cartilage and other joint tissues.

The major symptom of osteoarthritis is pain on movement of the affected joint. It hurts and grates—you can hear it. Except in severe cases, there is little or no pain in the resting state as there is in other arthritides. Because movement is painful, patients tend not to move, and after a while the range of motion that the joint can perform is seriously lessened. The simplest tasks become difficult to do—eating, writing, caring for one's self. Osteoarthritis at the hip is particularly difficult to manage—walking, dressing, sitting become mountainous problems.

Hands, the big toe, the knee, the hip, may become permanently deformed. *Nodes* or *nodules,* a kind of knot or knob, sometimes appear on osteoarthritic fingers and cause pain and redness, but these go away again. Bony swellings may enlarge the knee, and fluid may increase the swelling and may also result in a

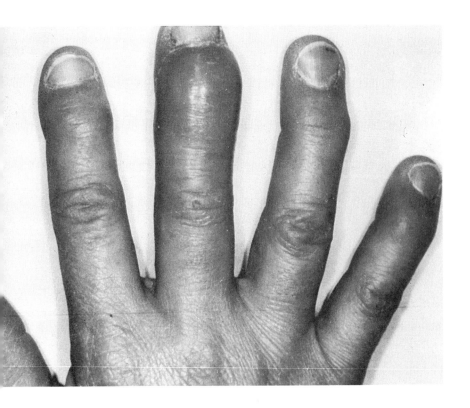

Nodes on all of the finger joints. These nodes are common in early stages of degenerative arthritis and usually disappear as the disease becomes chronic.

cyst—a sac that is filled with fluid and/or debris—that further reduces motion of the joint. Osteoarthritis at the hip can cause shortening of the leg at the affected joint, resulting in a bad limp. The osteoarthritic knee causes another kind of limp.

Osteoarthritis of the joints of the spine is called *spondylosis*. The joints degenerate, the weight of the body is supported incorrectly, and a true slipped-disk condition can result. In one form of spondylosis, there can be pressure from the bony processes of the vertebrae on blood vessels, nerve roots, and the spinal cord that can cause severe disability: pain, fainting, numbness, even small areas of paralysis.

A less serious form of spondylosis can occur in the cervical area of the spine, around the neck. Cervical spondylosis causes improper support of the head on the spine. Its causes are generally unknown, but one cause can be the quick back-and-forth motion of the head known as whiplash, such as sometimes occurs in the sudden stop of an automobile. If the site is more toward the head, cervical spondylosis causes headaches. If it is lower in the cervical area, the pain involves the shoulders and both arms and worsens on turning the neck. This spondylosis is not permanent, lasting anywhere from a few days to a few months.

Lumbar spondylosis is a common cause of back pain. It can also result in pressure on spinal nerve roots that sends pain down the back of the thigh and into the leg and foot, causing that well-known problem, sciatica, as it presses on the sciatic nerve. Sometimes, if pressure affects many nerve roots, severe weakness of the legs can occur, as well as loss of control over urine and bowels. Like cervical spondylosis, the lumbar version gradually improves. Unfortunately it can also recur.

Over the age of 50 most people have a spondylosis that results from overgrowth of the vertebrae. This is one of the major causes of "oh my aching back" complaints. In a few severe cases, there is a slipping of vertebrae that causes nerve damage as the vertebrae pinch the nerves of the spinal cord that run through them.

There are other spondyloses. They are inflammatory or infective in nature and are, therefore, properly called spondylitis, and are discussed in the following chapters.

CHAPTER

2

INFLAMMATORY ARTHRITIS

There are several arthritides characterized particularly by *inflammation,* a reaction of the tissues to injury that shows redness, heat, pain, and swelling of the affected part.

Rheumatoid Arthritis

Rheumatoid arthritis is second only to osteoarthritis in the number of its victims. It affects primarily the small joints in the hands and feet and the synovium, causing crippling deformities. This is an arthritis that usually starts in middle age or earlier. Estimates of the incidence of rheumatoid arthritis run as high as one person in every hundred, and females are two to three times as likely to suffer from it. It seems to start more in the winter and after some siege of sickness, but it is not considered an infective arthritis—one that comes as a result of infection elsewhere in the body.

What causes rheumatoid arthritis? Nobody knows for sure. There may be some hereditary trait, and there seems to be some connection to viral infections like German measles and serum hepatitis, the liver disease brought on by an injection of one kind or another. Because of this, scientists theorize that rheumatoid arthritis may be an *auto-immune* disease, one in which the body acts as though it were allergic to itself: in the battle against the viruses, the immune system somehow gets mixed up about what it is fighting and attacks normal joint tissue instead. And psychological elements, particularly stress, also seem to play some part in causing rheumatoid arthritis.

The patient with rheumatoid arthritis feels sick and feverish and has a lot of pain, with swelling and tenderness around the joints. But it may take as long as a year to confirm a diagnosis of rheumatoid arthritis. A blood test for what is called the ''rheumatoid factor'' is usually performed, but the test is not conclusive since a positive result can also point to other diseases. Other signs and symptoms finally develop that can confirm the diagnosis of rheumatoid arthritis. One such sign is the development of nodules in the skin, on bones and tendons, and at pressure points like the elbows and heels. X rays reveal *erosion*, wearing away, of bone at the edges of joints. Cartilage is damaged by the swelling caused when excess synovial fluid is produced in reaction to injury of the synovium. The ligaments weaken under the onslaught, so that the joint weakens and displaces or even dislocates. Or the opposite can happen: the breakdown of the fibers and bone can lead to a fusion of the joint so that it cannot bend.

Although some cases *remit*—disappear—in the first year, rheumatoid arthritis never gets cured. It comes and goes over the years, usually getting worse each time. Sometimes it can lead to one or more secondary problems like *anemia,* a condition in which there are not enough red blood cells to carry all the oxygen the body needs. The heart valves regulating the flow of blood to the body can be damaged, or those to the sac that protects the heart can become inflamed. There is also the possibility of respiratory tract complications, eye problems, and a heightened susceptibility to infection. These complications can make rheumatoid arthritis very serious indeed.

Polyarteritis Nodosa

Fortunately, this is a rare form of arthritis, for it can lead to complications that are dangerous to life. It affects four times as many males as females, mostly young adults. There is joint and muscle pain, nodules under the skin, ulcers or sores on the legs, and *gangrene*—death of the tissues—of the fingers and toes because of interrupted blood supply to those parts. The organs of the body are almost all involved, producing symptoms like sudden blindness, hemiplegia, and heart disease. Aggressive treatment prevents death, which at one time resulted within five years. Miraculously, some cases simply get better for no apparent reasons—called *spontaneous remission.*

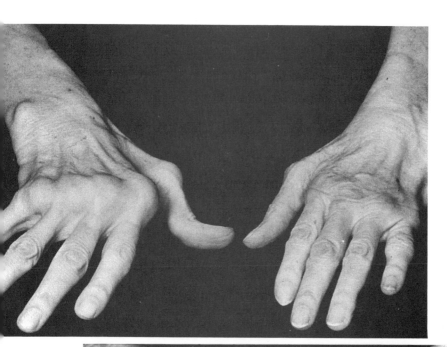
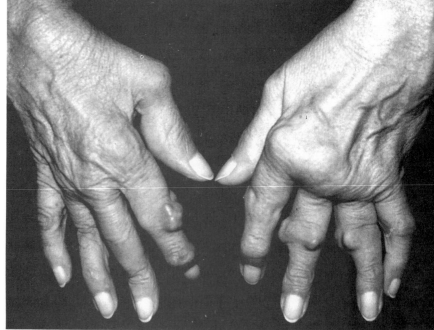

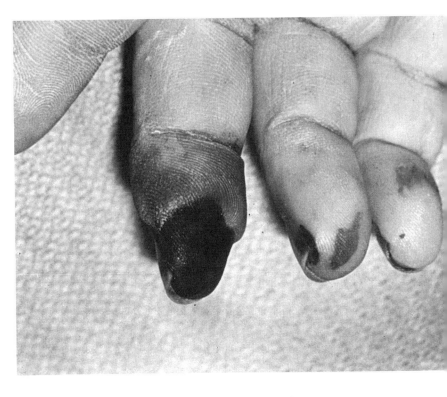

Above: *Gangrene—starting in the tips of the 4th and 5th fingers, more advanced in the middle finger*

Deformities of rheumatoid arthritis.
Top left: *The metacarpal joints, where fingers connect to hands, have displaced on the right hand. The hand is further disabled by the deviation, or sideward slant, of the fingers.* Bottom left: *Nodules, swelling due to excess synovial fluid, displacement of hand-finger joints. Nodules such as these tend to form on pressure points: below the elbow, the base of the spine, the Achilles tendon at the heel. They are most common in rheumatoid arthritis but also occur in lupus and polyarteritis nodosa.*

Ankylosing Spondylitis

This inflammatory arthritis of the spine causes *anky-losis*, fusing, of the vertebrae. It is more common in young men than women, and more common in the population than is generally realized. Statistics show that this condition may affect as many as one in every one hundred persons. There is an Indian tribe in Van-couver, Canada, in which over 6 percent of the pop-ulation suffers from ankylosing spondylitis, and this and other statistics show that there is a strong hered-itary element.

Ankylosing starts in the lower part of the spine and causes a mild stoop at first. As the vertebrae an-kylose further up the spine, the stoop gets more pro-nounced. If the ankylosis reaches the cervical verte-brae, the head bows and the body makes a *C*. Now the victim of ankylosing spondylitis can only look downward and within the field of eye movements. This constricted field increases the awkwardness of the person's gait, or manner of walking. Despite this dis-ability, function is usually good except for fatigue— it's tiring to struggle around this way. And sometimes the heart, stomach, and kidneys can be affected by the abnormal posture.

Still's Disease

Still's disease is often called juvenile rheumatoid ar-thritis. This is confusing. It is not a young form of rheumatoid arthritis, but is an inflammatory arthritis in juveniles.

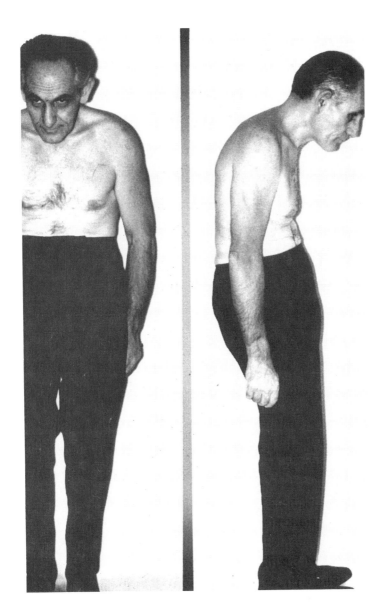

Advanced ankylosing spondylitis. Notice (left) how the patient must look upward in order to see ahead.

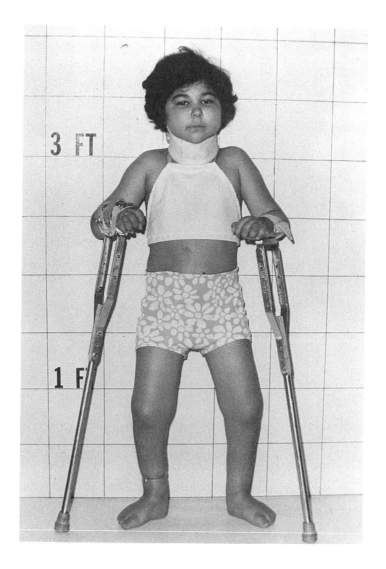

This 14-year-old patient with Still's disease is only 3'9" tall. She has shortened toes, fingers, and jaw. Neck and knee abnormalities require bracing. Her hip joints have rotated outward, and she needs crutches to assist walking.

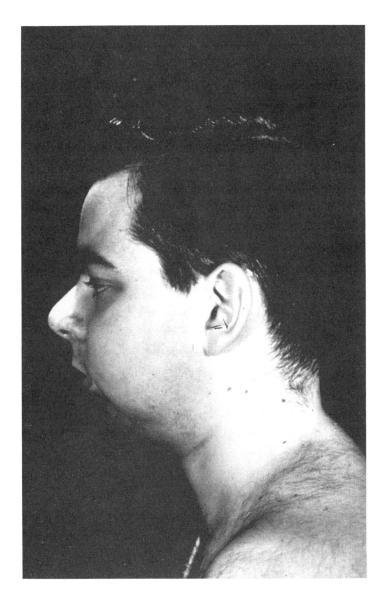

Receding chin, shortened lower jaw, and forward projection of head are typical in those who have had Still's disease for a long time.

This is a rare disease that can attack children to the age of 16, affecting growth of the limbs so that normal length in one or both legs may not be achieved. It also can cause eye diseases and even blindness. Although usually classified as an inflammatory arthritis, Still's disease may also be considered an infective arthritis (see the following chapter) because it is usually, but not always, secondary to infections like leukemia, rheumatic fever, sickle cell anemia, and other diseases.

One happy note: three out of four cases of Still's disease remit completely—often early enough for the child to catch up to normal or near-normal height.

CHAPTER

3

INFECTIVE ARTHRITIS

Infective arthritis is not infectious or contagious. People don't catch it. What you can catch is something that causes infection in your body that in turn causes arthritis. That something might be a bacterium, a virus, or a fungus.

Bacterial Infective Arthritis

A deep wound that penetrates a joint is a direct source of bacterial infection. But usually the infection is elsewhere, in a cut or abscessed teeth or boils, in a sickness caused by Staphylococcus, Streptococcus or Proteus bacteria. The arthritis these cause is accompanied by high fever and chills.

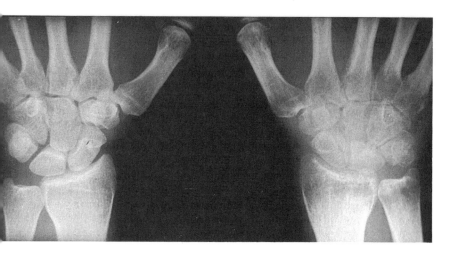

Staphylococcal arthritis in the right wrist has caused narrowing of many joints and irregularity of the borders of the bones. The left wrist is normal.

Gonorrhea, a *venereal* or sexually transmitted bacterial disease, can cause arthritis. Gonorrheal arthritis generally attacks only one or two joints but makes patients very sick, with a lot of pain, fever, and skin *lesions* or sores. *Syphilis,* a venereal disease that can progress through three stages of disability, often shows arthritis in the second and third stages.

Tubercular arthritis, secondary to tuberculosis, is particularly damaging to affected joints, often destroying them. Once most common in children, this arthritis faded when a cure for tuberculosis was found. Today, tuberculosis is on the rise again, and tubercular arthritis with it. But now the arthritis seems to be affecting more adults. The knees and hips are the joints most often affected, but these are not the only problem areas. Tubercular arthritis of the spine, called Pott's disease, is particularly disabling, and occurs in children and adults up to age 40. Destruction of the vertebrae causes a curvature of the spine as in spondylitis and can compress the nerves of the spinal cord and result in paralysis.

A form of *brucellosis,* like tuberculosis, can cause an infective arthritis that in rare cases can result in destruction of joints. Human brucellosis, also called *Malta fever,* comes from infected cows' milk and from other animal sources. Brucellosis is widespread in cattle, swine, and goats and is highly contagious among those lower animals. It rarely infects human beings, the highest species of animal, because we know how to protect ourselves from contact with the causative bacteria. Our milk supplies are carefully inspected and tested, and veterinarians are always checking for signs of brucellosis—and tuberculosis—in stock.

Lyme disease, or Lyme arthritis, is a fairly new disease in the world of medicine. It was first recognized and described in Lyme, Connecticut (thus its name!), only a few years ago. You will probably see newspaper articles about it every summer because that is usually when new cases appear, caused by the bite of a particular tick, carried by deer and field mice. These

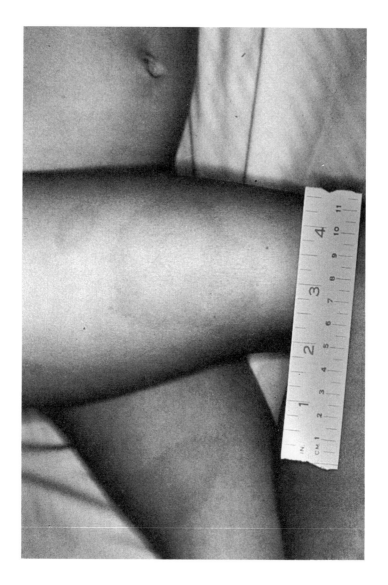

The first manifestation of Lyme disease (above rule).
The outer border is very red and flat, and the
inner part can be all red or sometimes turns bluish.

ticks in turn carry within their bodies a *spirochete,* a type of microorganism, that enters through the bite site. The result is a red bump that soon turns into one or more large lesions.

There is fever, headache, stiff neck, nervous system involvement, and heart symptoms. Arthritis of many joints may set in within several days—or it can occur up to two years after the bite. At first the arthritis is *acute*—starting rapidly and severely but not lasting long. In a few weeks or months it becomes *chronic*—long-lasting, drawn out, with few changes in condition, or repetitive.

Viral Infective Arthritis

Virus infections like rubella (German measles), mumps, some flu, and some upper-respiratory infections may sometimes bring on a temporary bout of arthritis or inflammation of the synovium. Viral hepatitis can also cause *arthralgia*, pain in the joints that is like arthritis. Only rarely does a true arthritis result from viral hepatitis.

Fungal Infective Arthritis

Fungal infections can cause an arthritis, but it is very rare because fungi do not seem to attack the skeletal system to any degree. When they do, other systems are also involved. The primary cause of fungal infective arthritis is the long-term antibiotic therapy used to combat the fungus.

CHAPTER

4

METABOLIC
AND MISCELLANEOUS
ARTHRITIDES

Few people think of gout as arthritis, but it is. Gout is usually considered the result of an excess of the "good life"—too much wine and rich foods. It is a problem caused by food, but not by food itself but by the way the body metabolizes food. *Metabolism* is the sum of all the physical and chemical changes that take place within an organism.

There are other arthritides that are not always recognized as such. They are gathered here under the "Miscellaneous" umbrella along with a few other arthritides that are not comfortably sheltered under previous umbrellas.

Metabolic Arthritis—Gout

For some strange reason, gout has always been laughed at—by everybody but those who suffer from it. Many is the old movie, like *Little Lord Fauntleroy,* that derides some crotchety old man with his heavily bandaged and protected foot propped up on a gout stool wielding his cane at anyone coming anywhere near him. And well he might, for that foot has a big toe with a giant pain that is exquisitely sensitive to touch.

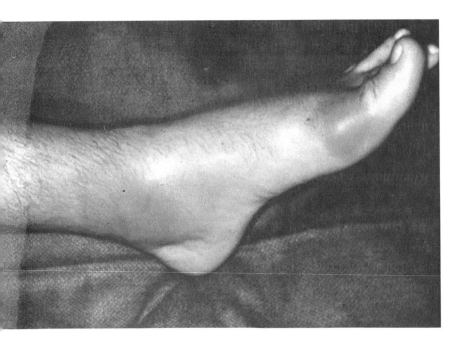

Even the picture of this gouty foot
looks painful! The big toe and the ankle
are red and swollen in an acute attack.

The urate crystals of gout seen under a
high-power microscope. These crystals are
almost always this fine needle shape.

Perhaps the lack of sympathy stems from the lo-
cation of the gout, that it is "only" the big toe causing what seems like excessive distress. Or perhaps it
was because gout was supposed to be brought on by
an overindulgence in port wine and served the sufferer right. That he had every right to be crotchety
did not seem to occur to anyone. Nor did anyone ever
picture the patient as a "she"—even today, when we
have much evidence to the contrary, gout is depicted
as a man's affliction. We also know that gout attacks
other joints than the big toe, in particular the knee and
the thumb.

One of the end products of the metabolism of
certain foods is uric acid, found normally in the urine.

Excessive uric acid stays in the bloodstream and crystallizes around the joints. These irritating chemical crystals cause gout, which is sometimes called a crystal arthritis. (They can also form kidney stones, exceedingly painful when they get jammed in the process of moving toward the bladder to be excreted from the body.)

Another form, *tophaceous gout,* shows deposits of *tophi*—a material that is the same as the tartar on your teeth—in joints, the outer ear, and around the fingernails.

The following are those arthritides that stand in a class by themselves, the ''miscellaneous class.''

Psoriatic Arthritis

Psoriasis is a common, inherited disease of the skin, a chronic condition that seems to be made worse by stress. Lesions of psoriasis may involve only a small area of the skin or, in its worst form, cover the entire body. When the skin is broken down over very large portions of the body, the internal temperature is affected, often resulting in high fevers, and the protection the skin gives against invading infections is lost. For some unknown reason psoriasis is accompanied about 7 percent of the time by its own form of arthritis. When the psoriasis gets worse, so does the arthritis. When the psoriasis improves, so does the arthritis—unless, as can happen, the joint has suffered too much damage. The hands particularly can be very disabled.

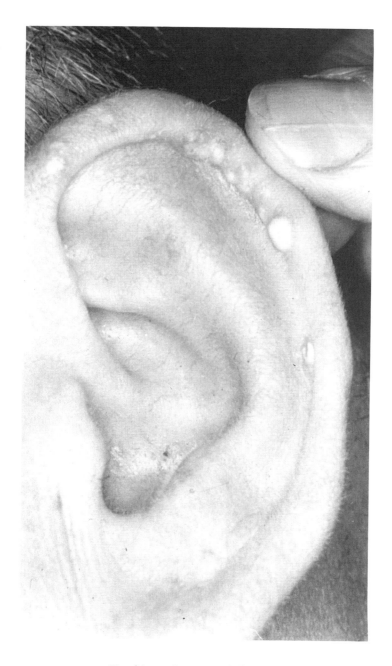

Tophi at the top of the ear

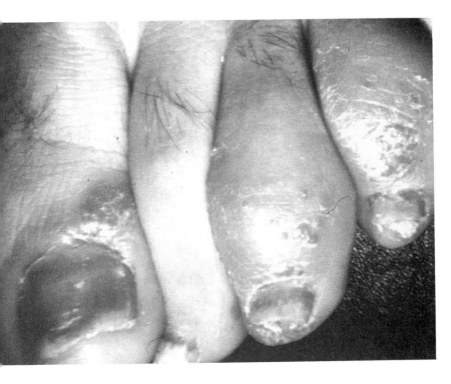

The 1st, 3rd, and 4th toes show psoriasis patches, and the joints of the 3rd and 4th toes are arthritic with what is known as "sausage" swelling.

There are drugs for both conditions, psoriasis and arthritis, but unfortunately, the drugs used to help the arthritis can make the skin worse. So treating the patient with psoriatic arthritis is a complicated matter of experimenting and adjusting. Sometimes psychotherapy is valuable in relieving underlying emotional problems and in helping the patient adjust to what can be a disfiguring disability.

Scleroderma (Systemic Sclerosis)

"Sclerosis" indicates hardening and "derma" skin, and scleroderma is a rare disease in which the skin becomes hard and leatherlike. But it is also a disease in which several organs other than the skin may harden, so it is often called systemic sclerosis, *systemic* indicating the body as a whole.

Many years ago, people thought of it as "turning to stone." This is not so, of course, but it can seem that way. As the skin hardens, the face may become fixed and masklike, the mouth cannot open fully, and the joints (particularly of the hands and feet) lose their range of motion and become arthritic. Posture and gait stiffen, and if ligaments and tendons of the joints harden, movement becomes an increasingly difficult problem. The hand can become rigid and clawlike, functionless. If the blood cannot circulate into the fingers and toes, gangrene results.

Some cases do not go beyond skin involvement. But when the disease involves the lungs, heart, and kidneys, these organs lose their ability to move and function, and death is inevitable. There have been cases which have remitted, but no one knows why, anymore than they know what caused the condition in the first place or how to cure it, although new drugs are helping delay its progress.

Systemic sclerosis occurs most often between the ages of twenty and fifty, but there is a form, confined to the skin, in infants and children. Four times as many women as men suffer from this disease, but white women and black men are more severely struck than

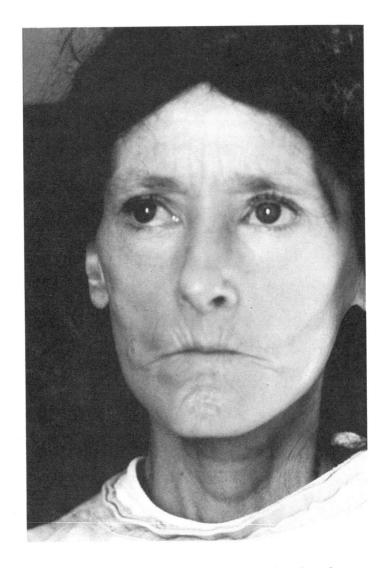

This is the face of a young woman with scleroderma. The muscles of the temple, face, and neck have atrophied, or shrunk; the lips are pursed; the skin is taut and shiny over cheeks and forehead. This is called "Mauskopf"—mousehead.

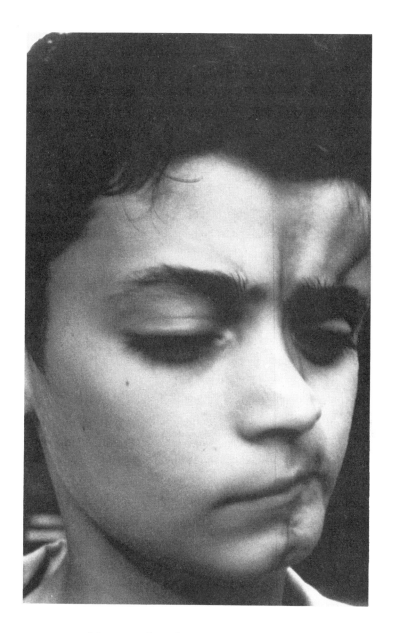

*Linear scleroderma—one-sided—
usually begins in adolescence.*

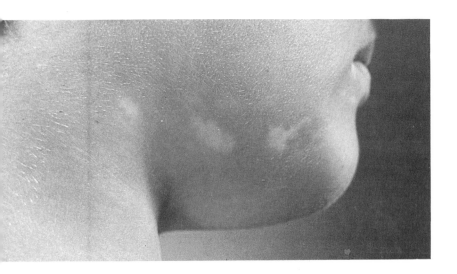

*Patches of sclerodermatous skin in
a child with localized scleroderma.
This form is called "morphea."*

black women and white men. This confusing distri-
bution of sex and race is another puzzle for researchers in systemic sclerosis.

Enteropathic Arthritis

Entero is a prefix indicating something intestinal. En-
teropathic arthritis is an arthritis that is associated with
intestinal diseases. It affects the large joints of the
lower limbs, then gradually disappears. Post-enteric
arthritis is really an infective arthritis, but it is classified here with its relative. This arthritis starts after a
gastrointestinal infection, particularly one caused by
the bacteria Salmonella.

Allergic Arthritis

That foods can cause an allergic reaction is well known. But the reaction is usually a rash or hives. That food *allergens*—allergy-causing substances—can cause an arthritis is a relatively new and not widely accepted concept. *Serum sickness,* the hypersensitivity to drugs, can also cause an allergic arthritis. (Auto-immune arthritis, which is an allergic reaction of the immune system to the body, is not included in this category.)

Fibromyalgia

Sometimes called "the great imposter," *fibromyalgia* has the same signs and symptoms as almost fifty other conditions. It attacks mostly (87 percent) women. Fibromyalgia is characterized by aches and pains in the bones and muscles all over the body, with many small, tender areas called *trigger points* that set off a reaction—pain—when touched. Often, sleep is disturbed when a turn or a toss touches off a trigger point. Changes in the weather seem to make symptoms worse, unlike most other forms of arthritis (contrary to folklore!). There is stiffness and aching, and often swelling or numbness of hands and feet. This may be an auto-immune condition or, as researchers are beginning to think, a chemical one. Scientists have discovered that a decrease in brain *serotonin,* a substance involved in transmitting impulses from one nerve to another, causes symptoms similar to those of fibromyalgia. It takes time and many tests to rule out other diseases before a diagnosis of fibromyalgia can be made.

The following are not always classified among the arthritides, but then again, sometimes they are—and they do show joint involvement.

Polymyalgia Rheumatica

This is a disease of the elderly, involving pain and severe stiffness in the shoulders and hips. It starts on one side first, then involves both sides. Polymyalgia rheumatica is sometimes confused with osteoarthritis because of the age of the patients and the fact that

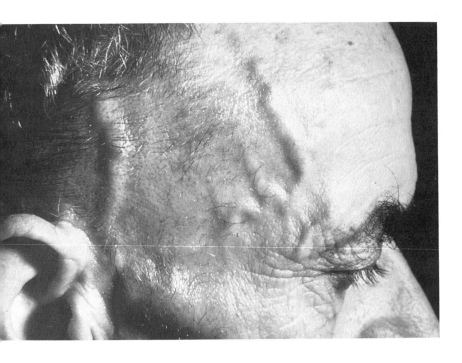

This bulging artery in the temporal region is a giant cell arteritis.

(58)

they might already have some osteoarthritis. But the stiffness is far more severe and may last for hours. Blood chemistry tests can confirm the diagnosis. Some patients show fever, suffer from loss of appetite, and appear so sick as to be at the point of death.

About 40 percent of the patients with polymyalgia rheumatica also have giant cell arteritis. This is a condition in which an artery in the brain becomes inflamed and blocked by giant cells that develop within it. Blood cannot flow through the blocked artery, causing death of the tissues the artery is meant to serve. If that artery serves the eye, blindness can result.

Bursitis

A *bursa* is a sac of synovial tissue over or between bones to help smooth motion. When a bursa becomes inflamed, from trauma or gout or another of the arthritides, you have *bursitis.* Bursitis occurs so often in the shoulder that many people think it's the only bursitis around. They just don't recognize that other equally well-known problems are also a bursitis. "Housemaid's knee" is a bursitis supposedly caused by kneeling to wash floors, but it can actually come from many activities involving the knee, or even spontaneously. A *bunion,* a greatly enlarged and displaced joint of the big toe, is another common bursitis people don't think of as bursitis.

Tenosynovitis

Tendons are protected by a tube of synovium surrounding them. Should a tube become inflamed, you have the swelling and pain of tenosynovitis. Tenosynovitis is fairly common in rheumatoid arthritis, but it is not restricted to those with other arthritic conditions. Repetitive or slightly awkward motions in the wrist and thumb are a common cause, and the palm side of the fingers or the web spaces between fingers are particularly subject to tenosynovitis. Tenosynovitis of the forefinger is known as "trigger finger," because it particularly affects target shooters who may pull the triggers of their guns for hours on end.

Shoulder Periarthritis

This is familiar as "frozen shoulder." It is caused by tendon degeneration in older people, or the rupture of a tendon because of trauma or a sudden overexertion of the shoulder. There is severe pain from the shoulder down the arm, often accompanied by stiffness, that can last for weeks or months.

Systemic Lupus Erythematosus

Called simply *lupus* by most people for obvious reasons (although then it becomes confused with another lupus, a skin disease), systemic lupus erythematosus is an auto-immune disease. It involves inflammation, so is sometimes categorized as inflammatory arthritis.

Lupus means "wolf" in Latin, and this disease can be wolflike in the way it preys on the organs of its victims. Flannery O'Connor, the famous author, died of it. Shortly before her death she wrote in a letter, "The wolf, I'm afraid, is tearing up the place."

Lupus is a disease that attacks from childhood on, though it is found mostly in the 20- to 40-year-old woman. It starts in almost every case with an arthritis that affects most of the joints and can go on to attack the organs of the body: (in order of frequency) the skin, kidneys, lymph glands, heart, lungs, liver, spleen, and brain. A skin rash, or *erythema,* often runs across the nose and under the eyes in a butterfly shape.

Cases of systemic lupus erythematosus range from mild to severe, and there are times when symptoms disappear for considerable lengths of time. Yesterday many cases of lupus were fatal. Today, there are drugs that can keep the wolf at bay.

Rheumatic Fever

This is a disease that is sometimes grouped with rheumatoid arthritis and the inflammatory arthritides. However, it is not an arthritis itself but has arthritis as a major symptom. It is rare before the age of 5 or after 18. There can be recurrent attacks of rheumatic fever over the years. Like lupus, it is a disease that can affect the heart and skin as well as the joints. Inflammation of the heart and congestive heart disease are common, and arthritis moves about the joints, attacking first one and then another. But sometimes there is no joint involvement at all, and sometimes the symptoms as a whole are so mild they are not reported to a doctor or not diagnosed as rheumatic fever. Only when heart-valve damage shows up in adulthood is a diagnosis made.

(61)

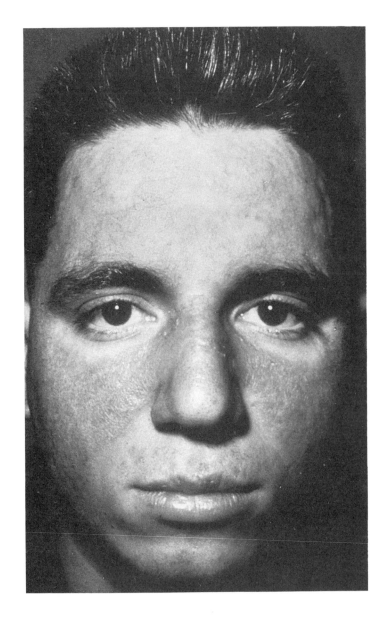

The butterfly rash of lupus. There is also a finer rash around the mouth and on the forehead.

It's a puzzle to researchers, and the cause of rheumatic fever is still unknown. What is known is that rheumatic fever occurs after infection with a strain of microorganism called streptococci A. This is the strep that causes "strep throat." But strep infections are common, and only rarely do they go on to rheumatic fever. So something else is working along with the strep to cause the disease, and that something else is what researchers need to find out about.

Reiter's Disease

This disease was named by a German army doctor in World War I, Hans Reiter, who encountered many cases of it among troops, particularly after bouts of *dysentery,* severe diarrhea. This is a disease of young men, with three sets of symptoms: arthritis, *urethritis* (inflammation of the urethra, the tube in the penis carrying urine and semen), and *conjunctivitis (pink eye,* or inflammation of the lining of the eyelids). The arthritis attacks a few large joints and causes painful heels and breakdown of the skin of the feet and sometimes the nails. This is not a disease confined to military troops—quite a number of young adults seem to get it.

There are a few more arthritides, components of very rare conditions, about which there is little to say but that they exist, and they cause pain and disability. Arthritis in any of its forms is a cruel burden. Pain and disability are difficult to cope with, yet billions

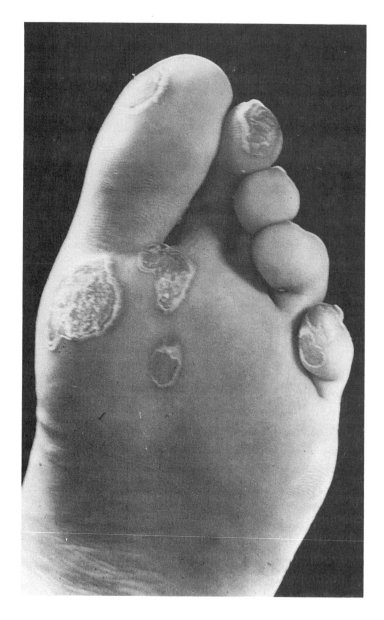

*Rash and pustules on the side
of the foot in Reiter's disease*

of arthritis sufferers do so, and most of them quite successfully. What treatments are there? How do they care for themselves and their families? Of course, everyone is different, everyone has his or her own problems, everyone makes his or her own adjustment to them. But these are not unique problems or adjustments, and we can consider them as a group without making less of them—remembering all the while that we are talking about people, about ourselves.

CHAPTER

5

COPING

The pitchman stands by the side of his gaudily decorated wagon, waving a bottle in the air. "Good for everything that ails you, and things that don't, too!" The audience laughs appreciatively and listens attentively to his sales talk, his pitch, ready to believe that whatever is in his bottle will cure them of whatever ailment or problem they have. "Seneca Oil," "Genesee Ointment," "Snake Oil," "ancient Indian formula,"—rub it in or drink it down or both. . . . The audience swarms to buy this magic potion that will make their aches and pains disappear.

Most of those pains came from arthritis, and in the 19th century these pitchmen and medicine shows covered the country. They offered hope, if nothing else. Some of the ointments were pure petroleum, an old Indian standby, a black oily substance they scooped up from mysterious shallow pools in the forests. (We still make medicines from by-products of the processes that turn petroleum into gasoline.) Some liniments were mostly colored water and alcohol—if rubbing them into an aching spot didn't help, drinking it would make you forget the pain for a while.

The medicine shows are gone, but there are still pitchmen around hawking their arthritis remedies, although today they use newspapers and TV. Their "cures" are just as meaningless as those offered a hundred years ago, maybe more so. Copper bracelets, crystals, honey and vinegar, herb teas, "special" muds, "special" waters, "special" baths, "special" wraps. . . . Even a spray meant for easing stiff locks has had a following among some arthritis sufferers who apparently hope that stiff human joints will respond to it. It's not that these things don't work to relieve pain for a little while. They may, if you believe in them, if they soothe your mind or your body or give you hope. A stay at a spa, with its constant attentions and little luxuries, can make anyone feel better in every way. Some rubs or wraps create a soothing warmth that can ease pain for a while; some can help ease the way pain is perceived.

Pain is interpreted in receptors in the brain that receive nerve impulses traveling from the source of the pain. Those perceptions can sometimes be altered by conscious effort, by the willing of it. TM (transcendental meditation) or hypnosis or *biofeedback,* a training system to develop the ability to control the involuntary nervous system of the body, may help to change the perception of chronic pain. Acupuncture may work in this way, or it may have a purely physical effect—no one is quite sure. But acupuncture has been successful in relieving the pain of arthritis. Its effects are short-lived, however, and acupuncture needs to be repeated at frequent intervals, sometimes weekly.

Treatment for arthritis depends on the symptoms and varies with the physician, who may be a *rheumatologist* (specialist in rheumatic diseases), an *orthopedist* (a specialist in problems of the musculoskeletal system), a *physiatrist* (specialist in physical medicine), or a general practitioner. But there are some specifics. Surgery can be performed on vertebrae to relieve the exaggerated stoop of spondylitis or to remove the bone growth pressing on nerves in spondylosis. An arthritic knee or hip joint can be replaced with an artificial joint that works amazingly well, particularly in the hip, and relieves limping and pain. Bunions can be surgically removed, ligaments repaired, offending bony growths or calcifications removed. Of course, not everyone can undergo the trauma of surgery. The elderly, the overweight, the diabetic, the patient with heart or lung disease face more danger from surgery than from arthritis. And not many arthritic conditions benefit from surgery.

Anti-inflammatory substances are administered when the joints show inflammation. *Corticosteroids*— substances derived from hormones produced in the cortex (outer layer) of the adrenal gland—are often used to reduce inflammation. Direct injection into an inflamed bursa or joint or synovial tissue helps relieve pain in traumatic arthritis, bursitis, and the acute stages

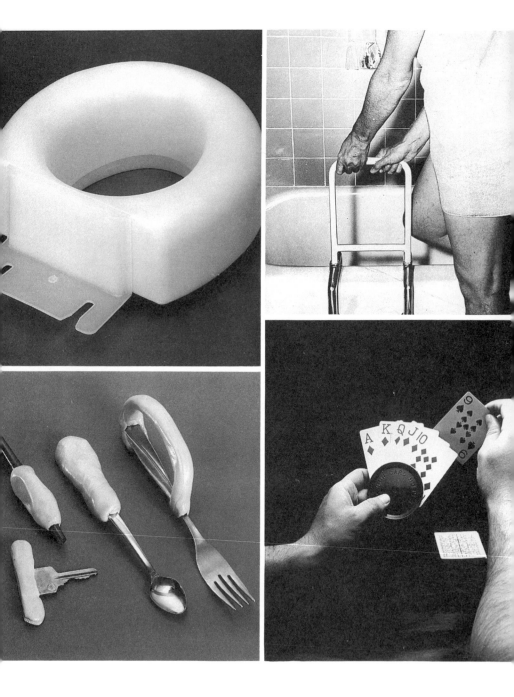

Reprinted by permission of © J.A. Preston Corporation 1989

Different kinds of adapted equipment make living easier for arthritic patients: A.) Raised toilet seat. B.) Bathtub grab bar. C.) Arthritic fingers can get a better grip on built-up handles. There are many different kinds of handles that can be bought or made to suit the individual patient's needs. D.) Recreation is important, too, and this cardholder helps the patient with arthritic hands. E.) This reacher gets things down from high shelves and picks things up off floors. F.) Arthritic hips make getting out of chairs difficult. This cushion, called a lifter seat, helps by pneumatic action.

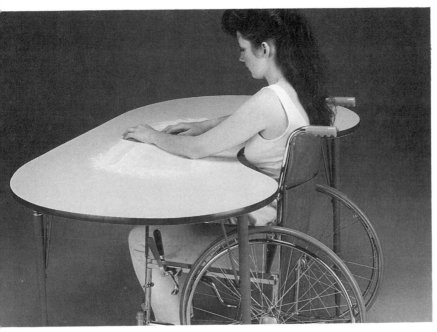

*Assistive exercise helps in non-acute arthritis.
Here the elbow is assisted by moving on a surface
made friction-free with powder.*

of the inflammatory arthritides. But the side effects of
steroids on other organs of the body limit their use.
A typical "moon face," round, puffy, and with flat-
tened features, is the sign of heavy steroid administra-
tion. In children, growth can be stunted by steroids.
Other anti-inflammatory agents are drugs like ibupro-
fen and indomethacin, and gold. Yes, gold—that yel-
low metal. Instead of trying to turn salt into gold,
today's alchemists turn gold into a salt form and use

it as an anti-inflammatory agent in early rheumatoid arthritis and some cases of lupus and osteoarthritis.

The first consideration in every arthritis is to relieve pain. The *analgesic*—pain reliever—most used is aspirin (or one of aspirin's relatives as advertised on TV). Heat in any form—baths, soaks, electric heating pads, warm paraffin (a derivative of that old Genesee oil, petroleum)—is an analgesic, as are a growing army of medications. And whatever helps the underlying conditions of some arthritides, like psoriasis and food allergies and venereal diseases and tuberculosis, will also help the arthritides they involve.

Most arthritides have no sure cure, and in those cases therapy is directed toward making the patient more comfortable and more functional. Disability, pain, and deformity change one's self-image and cause major changes in life-style. The person who has been independent and finds that arthritis has limited that independence needs to bring great powers to bear to adjust mentally as well as physically. Social and economic standing may change. The disabled worker may have to give up a good income and manage on paltry insurance benefits. Mobility, the ability to travel, can be limited. Driving a car or using the steps of a bus or train may be impossible, keeping the arthritis sufferer from normal contacts and relationships. Periods of hospitalization add to this sense of isolation, of separation from the world. Hospitals are abnormal environments, and prolonged stays can lead to psychological problems, particularly for youngsters.

Young people fall behind in school if absences are prolonged or repeated, although homebound

*Stress plays a part in arthritis, as in every disease,
and is important to recognize and overcome.*

teachers are usually provided. That doesn't help in the fun things of school: the clubs, the teams, the socializing. The youngster with arthritis worries about making friends if he or she has a limp or a hand deformity or needs to rest a lot. It isn't easy to care for toileting or menstrual needs or to do something as simple as holding a glass of milk. Some people give up. They let themselves be taken care of, often they demand it, tyrannizing over their families. Others realize that the only way to improve their state is to work at it, to strive for the best function possible. It's not something that the doctor gives a shot for. But there are many improvements in condition that patients can effect for themselves.

There are special programs to help. Most are based in out-patient hospital clinics in departments of physical medicine. Therapists also go into the home to work with patients. Physiatrists (not to be confused with psychiatrists!) prescribe rehabilitation programs of physical and occupational therapy. They might ask the occupational therapist to make a resting splint to keep an inflamed part from moving, or an active splint to assist movement. Therapists provide assistance with walking or using affected joints to increase their range of motion and to make the muscles stronger. Diathermy, a high-frequency current, is sometimes used to deliver deep heat to an arthritic joint. Heat is also used in other forms, like paraffin baths into which the parts are repeatedly dipped to build up a long-lasting waxy coating of warmth.

When arthritic joints hurt or are inflamed, it is difficult to move them, and they can stiffen and be-

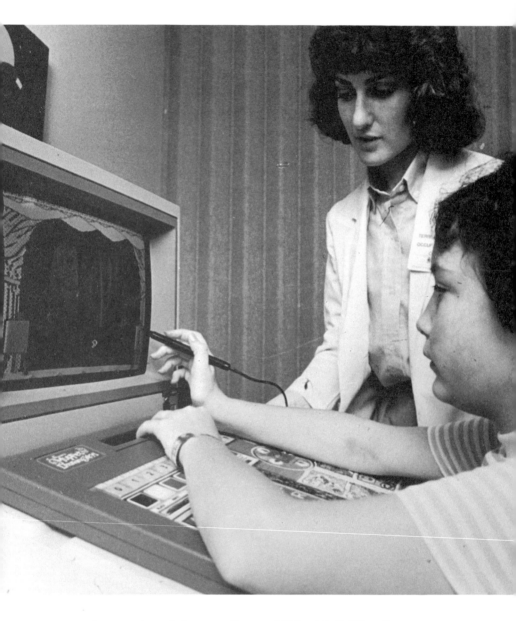

Occupational therapy for a child with Still's disease increases motion in hands and arms.

come incapable of movement. A physical therapist can gently move the joints for the patient, called "passive motion," so that they do not freeze up. When inflammation has passed, "active motion," motion the patient does for himself or herself, is encouraged so that the range of motion of the joint is extended to as close to normal as possible. The occupational and physical therapists offer activities for the most movement possible from the joints, striving to increase it. The occupational therapist also specializes in helping with what is called "activities of daily living," those things we all need to do to get through the day. Arthritic patients can have lots of problems with activities the rest of the world takes for granted, like getting in and out of bathtubs, beds, and chairs; getting on and off toilets; getting into and out of clothes; cooking, opening cans, sewing, using a toothbrush or a pen. . . . The list of activities of daily living can go on for pages, and any number of them can be a problem.

Fortunately, most problems have solutions. Toilet seats can be raised with a seat attachment. Beds and bathtubs can be made easier to get in and out of with strategically placed handles called "grab bars" to hold onto. Handles of cooking utensils and hairbrushes and toothbrushes can be built up so that fingers do not have to close too tightly on them. There are a large number of gadgets to adapt pens and pencils to arthritic fingers. There are devices to assist in putting on socks, stockings, and panty hose. Velcro can be used to replace difficult fastenings like buttons and shoelaces, ties can be bought pre-knotted, and many other adaptations can be made or bought.

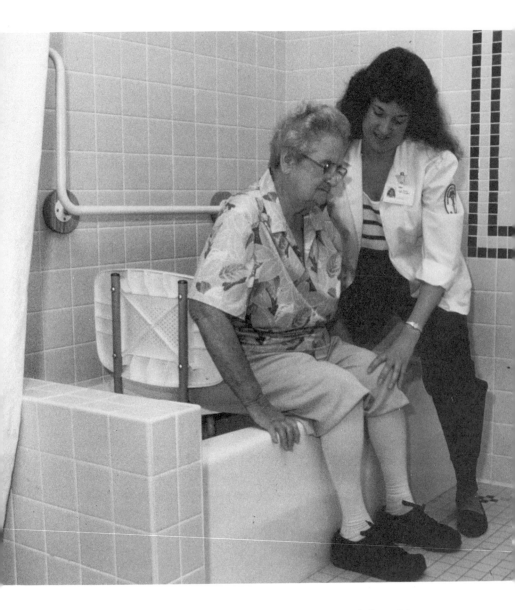

*Bars to hold on to and a seat to sit in while taking
a shower are important for the arthritic patient—but
first you have to learn how to get in and out.*

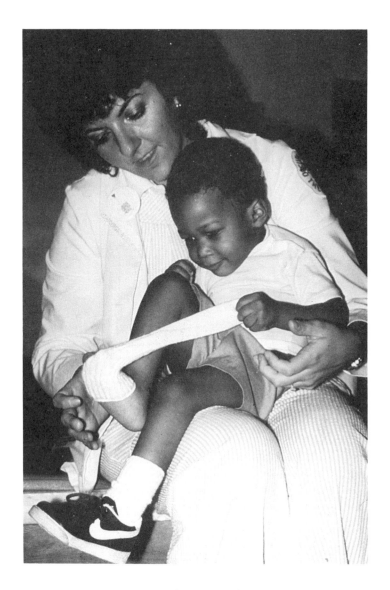

*Putting on your socks or stockings by yourself
is important. Young children who are living in the
unnatural setting of a hospital need help not
only with socks but also with developing normally.*

For some people, using adapted equipment is easy. They're glad to have anything that can help them. Others find it embarrassing to use canes or splints, or special forks and knives, or other equipment. Mental health professionals and the physical medicine team help with these feelings and adjustments. There are many other support groups and behavior modification groups.

Various helping organizations (see the list at the end of the book) provide support and up-to-date information on medications and everything else of concern to the arthritis patient and his or her family, including how-to tips for making life easier and more rewarding despite disability. The school or public library is another source of information.

A disability need not be a handicap—it becomes one only when there is loss of function. Many concerned hands are out there to help keep that loss to a minimum.

GLOSSARY AND PRONUNCIATION GUIDE

Acute (uh-kewt′). Starting rapidly and severely; not long-lasting.

Allergens (al′-er-jenz). Substances that cause allergic reactions.

Analgesic (ann-al-gee′-zic). Pain reliever.

Anemia (uh-neem′-yuh). Condition of too few red blood cells to carry all the oxygen the tissues of the body need.

Ankylosis (ang-key-low′-siss). Fusing.

Arthralgia (arth-ral′-juh). Pain in the joints.

Arthritis (arth-right′-iss). Inflammation of a joint and of the tissues surrounding the joint. Pl. *arthritides* (arth-rit′-ih-deez).

Articular cartilage (ar-tick′-you-ler car′-til-lej). Firm, jellylike substance that cushions most joints.

Auto-immune (auto-im-mewn′). Reaction in which body acts as if allergic to itself.

Biofeedback. Training system to develop ability to control involuntary nervous system of body, which normally functions unconsciously.

Brucellosis (brew-cell-oh′-sis). A disease primarily of lower animals that can be transmitted to human beings, causing, among other symptoms, a bacterial infective arthritis. Also known in humans as Malta fever.

Bunion (bun'-yun). A greatly enlarged and displaced joint of the big toe.

Bursa (burr'-suh). Sac of synovial tissue over or between bones to help smooth motion.

Bursitis (burr-sight'-us). Condition of inflammation of a bursa.

Cartilage. See Articular cartilage.

Chronic (kron'-ick). Long-lasting, drawn out, with few changes in condition, or repetitive.

Conjunctivitis (kon-junk-ti-vy'-tiss). Pink eye, or inflammation of the lining of the eyelids.

Corticosteroids (kor'-tick-oh-steer'-oydz). Anti-inflammatory substances derived from hormones produced in the cortex (outer layer) of the adrenal gland.

Cyst (sist). A sac within the body filled with fluid and/or debris.

Disk. See Intervertebral disk.

Dysentery (dis'-en-terry). Severe diarrhea.

Entero (en-terr'-oh). Relating to the intestines.

Erosion (iroh'-zhun). Wearing away.

Erythema (er-i-theem'-uh). A form of rash that shows as a redness.

Femur (fee'-mur). Thighbone.

Fibromyalgia (figh'-broh-my-al'-juh). Condition characterized by aches and pains in muscles and joints over the entire body.

Gangrene (gang-reen'). Death of tissue in the body, usually due to lack of blood supply.

Gonorrhea (gon-or-ee'-uh). Sexually transmitted bacterial disease.

Hemiplegia (hemi-plee'-zhuh). Paralysis of one side of the body.

Immune system (im-mewn'). Automatic body response to internal attack.

Inflammation. A condition of the body characterized by redness, tenderness, heat, and swelling. Usually secondary to trauma. *See* Trauma.

Intervertebral disc (in-ter-ver-tee'-brul disk). Cartilage cushion between the vertebrae of the spine. *See also Articular cartilage.*

Joint. The place where two bones meet or "articulate."

Lesions (lee'-zhuhns). Sores.

Ligament (lig'-uh-ment). Sheet of fibrous connective tissue that binds the ends of bones in a joint and thickens into a capsule that surrounds the joint to help protect it.

Lupus erythematosus, systemic (lew'-pus er-i-theema-toh'-sis sistem'-ick). Chronic inflammatory disease of unknown cause that affects joints and organs of the body, usually with erythema in butterfly shape on face. *See* Erythema.

Malta fever. See Brucellosis.

Metabolism (met-tab'-oh-lizm). Sum of all the physical and chemical changes that take place within an organism.

Muscle (mus'-sull). Tissue made of cells or fibers that can contract (tighten) or relax (return to their original state).

Nervous system. The brain and spinal cord with its nerves and connections that receive messages and transmit them into actions.

Nodes. Knot or knobs under the skin.

Nodules (nah'-djewls). *See* Nodes.

Orthopedist (orth-oh-pee'-dist). Physician specializing in treating problems of the musculoskeletal system.

Osteo (ahs'-tee-oh). Prefix meaning bone.

Physiatrist (fizz-eye'-at-rist). Physician specializing in rehabilitation medicine.

Pink eye. See Conjunctivitis.

Polyarthritis. Arthritis in more than one joint of the body.

Psoriasis (sore-eye'-uh-sis). Skin disease which is sometimes accompanied by its own form of arthritis.

Remit (ree-mitt'). Disappear. *See also* Spontaneous remission.

Rheumatism (roo'-mat-izm). Those conditions involving inflammation of the bone and the tissues surrounding the bone: muscle, tendons, ligaments, cartilage, and fibrous connective tissue.

Rheumatologist (roo-mat-ol'-oh-jist). Physician specializing in treating rheumatic diseases.

Serotonin (sera-toe'-nin). Substance in brain that is involved in transmitting impulses from one nerve to another.

Serum sickness (seer'-um). Hypersensitivity to drugs.

Spirochete (spy'-row-keet). A microorganism.

Spondylosis (spahn-di-low'-sis). Fusing of vertebrae.

Spontaneous remission. Sudden disappearance of symptoms for no apparent reason.

Synovium, synovial tissue, synovial membrane (sin-oh'-vee-um, sin-oh'-vee-ul). Clear, thick, sticky fluid that smoothes movement of joints.

Syphilis (siff'-i-liss). An infectious disease transmitted sexually that may have arthritis as a symptom.

Systemic (sis-tem'-ik). Pertaining to the body as a whole, rather than one part.

Systemic lupus erythematosus. See Lupus erythematosus, systemic.

Tendon. Fibrous connective tissue band that attaches skeletal muscle to a joint.

Tophaceous gout (toe-fashe'-us gowt). Form of gout characterized by deposits of tophi. *See* Tophi.

Tophi (toe'-fee). Stony deposit, tartar on teeth.

Trauma (trow'-muh). Shock or injury.

Trigger point. Place on the body which, when touched, is painful.

Urethritis (your-eeth-right'-iss). Inflammation of the urethra, tube from bladder to outside of body.

Venereal (ven-ear'-ee-ul). Sexually transmitted.

Vertebra (ver'-teh-bra). Bone of spine. Pl. *vertebrae* (ver'-teh-bray).

FOR FURTHER INFORMATION

The American Lupus Society
23751 Madison St.
Torrance, California 90505

Arthritis Foundation
1314 Spring St., NW
Atlanta, Georgia 30309
(Local branches are listed in telephone books.)

American Academy of Physical Medicine
and Rehabilitation
30 N. Michigan Ave.
Chicago, Illinois 60602

American Occupational Therapy Association
1383 Piccard Drive
Rockville, Maryland 20850

American Physical Therapy Association
1156 15th St., NW
Washington, DC 20005

Arthritis Information Clearinghouse
POB 9782
Arlington, Virginia 22209
(A government agency that acts as a
referral center but has some publications.)

Canadian Arthritis and Rheumatism Society
45 Charles St.
E. Toronto, Ontario, Canada

Lupus Foundation of America
4801 W. Peterson Ave.
Chicago, Illinois 60646

The National Institute of Arthritis and
Musculoskeletal and Skin Diseases
9000 Rockville Pike
Building 31, Room 9A04
Bethesda, Maryland 20892
(One of the federal government's National
Institutes of Health. Supports multipurpose
arthritis centers around the country.
Publications and tapes, information about
community services.)

Scleroderma Federation, Inc.
1725 York Ave.
New York, New York 10128

Local Ys offer self-help courses including
water therapy and pain relief as well as
relaxation techniques.

State and city departments of health,
medical centers, and libraries have
up-to-date information.

(86)

Particularly for Young People

Stanford University Multipurpose Arthritis Center
101 Welch Rd., Suite 3301
Stanford, California 94304
(Audiovisual materials re: stress management
and relaxation techniques.)

"You Have Arthritis Coloring Book"
University of Missouri Medical Center
Columbia, Missouri 65212

INDEX

Malta fever (brucellosis), 43
"Mauskopf," *54*
Metabolic arthritis, 47, *48,*
 48–50, *49*
Metabolism, 47
"Morphea," *56*
Mumps, 45
Muscles, 13

Nervous system, 21
Nodes/nodules, 18, *28,* 32,
 33, *34*
Numbness, 29

Occupational therapy, 75, *76,*
 77
O'Connor, Flannery, 60
Orthopedist, 69
Osteoarthritis, 58–59, 73
 causes of, 25, 27
 at hip, 28–29
 of spine (spondylosis),
  29–30
 symptoms of, 27–39
Osteoporosis, 27

Paget's disease, 25, *26,* 27
Pain, 27, 29, 42, 45, 48, 60
 analgesic for, 73, 75
 perception of, 68–69
 trigger points of, 57
Paraffin bath, 73, 75
Paralysis, 29, 43
"Passive motion," 77
Periarthritis, shoulder, 60
Perthes' disease, 27
Physiatrists, 75
Physical therapy, 72, 75, 77
Pink eye, 63

Polyarteritis nodosa, 33, 36
Polymyalgia rheumatica, *58,*
 58–59
Post-enteric arthritis, 56
Pott's disease, 43
Pressure points, 32, *34*
Proteus bacteria, 41
Psoriasis, 50, 52, *52*
Psychiatrist, 69
Psychotherapy, 52

Reiter, Hans, 63
Reiter's disease, 63, *64*
Remit, 33, 40, 53
Rheumatic fever, 40, 61, 63
Rheumatism, 11–12, 17, 25
Rheumatoid arthritis, 31–33,
 34, 60, 61, 73
"Rheumatoid factor," 32
Rheumatologist, 69
Rubella (German measles),
 32, 45

Salmonella, 56
Sciatica, 29
Scleroderma (systemic scle-
 rosis), 53, *54, 55, 56,* 56
Serotonin, 57
Serum sickness, 57
Shoulder:
 frozen (periarthritis), 60
 stiffness in, 58
Sickle cell anemia, 40
Skeletal muscle, 13
Skin:
 erythema, 61, *62*
 hardening (scleroderma),
  53, *54, 55, 56,* 56
 See also Lesions

"Slipped disk," 17, 29
Smooth muscle, 13
Spine, 17
  ankylosing spondylitis,
    36
  curvature of, 43
  osteoarthritis
    (spondylosis), 29–30
  tubercular arthritis (Pott's
    disease), 43
  See also Vertebrae
Spirochete, 45
Spondylitis, ankylosing, 36,
  37, 69
Spondylosis, 29–30, 69
Spontaneous remission, 33
Staphylococcus, 41
Steroids, 72
Still's disease, 36, 38, 39,
  40, 76
Strep infection, 63
Streptococcus, 41, 63
Surgery, 69
Synovial fluid, 32
Synovial membrane, 16
Synovial tissue, 69
Synovium, 16, 32
Syphilis, 42
Systemic sclerosis (sclero-
  derma), 53, 54, 55, 56, 56

Tendon, 13, 16, 59, 60

Tenosynovitis, 59–60
Ticks, 43, 45
TM (transcendental
  meditation), 68
Toe:
  bunion, 58, 69
  gout, 48, 48–49
Tophaceous gout, 50, 51
Tophi, 50, 51
Trauma, as cause of
  osteoarthritis, 27
"Trigger finger," 60
Trigger points, 57
Tubercular arthritis, 42–43
Tuberculosis, 42

Ulcers, 33
Urethritis, 63
Uric acid, 49, 49–50

Velcro, 77
Venereal disease, 42
Vertebrae, 29
  fusing, 36
  invertebral disks, 17
  overgrowth, 30
  slipping, 30
  See also Spine
Viral infective arthritis, 45
Virus, 41

Whiplash, 29